W9-BWC-130

21st Century Skills **INNOVATION** *Library*

Football

by Jim Gigliotti

Published in the United States of America by Cherry Lake Publishing
Ann Arbor, Michigan
www.cherrylakepublishing.com

Content Adviser: Thomas Sawyer, EdD, Professor of Recreation and Sport Management, and
Physical Education, Indiana State University

Design: The Design Lab

Photo Credits: Cover and page 3, ©NRT-Sports/Alamy; page 5, ©AP Photo/Matt Slocum; pages
6, 9, 11, 12, 22, and 25, ©AP Photo; page 15, ©Houndstooth Archive/Alamy; page 16, ©Gary
Paul Lewis, used under license from Shutterstock, Inc.; page 18, ©iStockphoto.com/Kameleon007;
page 19, ©iStockphoto.com/gpflman; page 20, ©AP Photo/Charlie Neibergall; page 27, ©AP
Photo/Julian Wilson; page 28, ©AP Photo/File

Library of Congress Cataloging-in-Publication Data
Gigliotti, Jim.
 Football / by Jim Gigliotti.
    p. cm.—(Innovation in sports)
 Includes index.
 ISBN-13: 978-1-60279-257-9
 ISBN-10: 1-60279-257-7
 1. Football—Juvenile literature. I. Title. II. Series.
 GV950.7.G54 2009
 796.332—dc22   2008002305

Cherry Lake Publishing would like to acknowledge the work of
The Partnership for 21st Century Skills.
Please visit www.21stcenturyskills.org *for more information.*

CONTENTS

CHAPTER ONE

Football History

Imagine you are growing up in the 1870s. You hear about a sport called football. You want to see what it is about, so you go to a game between Yale and Princeton universities. You watch as a bunch of players surround one player with the ball. The entire pile of players moves up and down the dirt-brown field. The players wear heavy, dark uniforms made of canvas and wool.

Now fast-forward more than 125 years. You go to see a National Football League (NFL) game between the New England Patriots and the Dallas Cowboys. The two teams feature sophisticated offenses that pass the ball a lot. It's a fast-paced, well-polished game played between teams in colorful uniforms on a bright green field.

How did football get from there to here?

The modern game of football is as much about strategy as it is about power. In this game, the Dallas Cowboys play the New England Patriots.

The **innovations** of the game have allowed football to develop from its European roots into an American game. These innovations have come in many different areas—from the rules of the game to the equipment that the players use—and much more.

In the 1880s, athletic clubs began forming in big cities everywhere. Each of those athletic clubs had a football team. Each club wanted to be better at football than the other clubs. At first, clubs used only **amateur**

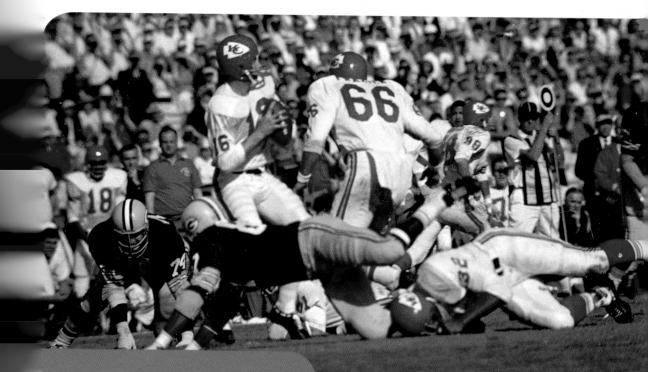

The Kansas City Chiefs and the Green Bay Packers played in the world's first Super Bowl in January 1967. The Packers won.

players. Soon clubs began paying men to play on
their teams.

By the 1890s, **professional** football players were
hitting the field. Regional leagues were formed. Many of
these leagues were located in Ohio. But they were loosely
organized. So in 1920, in an automobile showroom in
Canton, Ohio, a group of men got together and formed
the American Professional Football Association. That
organization eventually became known as the NFL.

NFL games have become a favorite spectator sport
in America. But it took a while for the NFL to get to
that level. For a long time, pro football took a backseat
to college football and Major League Baseball, in the
eyes of sports fans. That began to change when television
became a fixture in American households. The action
of a football game fit perfectly on a television screen.
Millions of viewers began tuning in to watch their
favorite teams.

In January 1967, another development helped the
NFL explode in popularity—the first Super Bowl was
played. The Super Bowl came about after a rival league,
the American Football League (AFL), began competing
with the NFL in 1960. The AFL began recruiting great
players out of college. The AFL also gained the attention
of the **media** and football fans. After several years of
fighting, the two leagues decided they would be better

For many years, the Super Bowl has been televised in dozens of countries around the world. But in the 21st century, the NFL started playing regular-season games on international soil. The first step was when the Arizona Cardinals played the San Francisco 49ers in Mexico City in 2005. Then, in 2007, the New York Giants and the Miami Dolphins played the first regular-season game ever held overseas, in London, England. NFL commissioner Roger Goodell says that the league is exploring the possibility of one day playing the Super Bowl on foreign soil. The NFL hopes that it can one day be considered a global game.

off together. The championship game between the leagues became known as the Super Bowl.

Beginning with the 1970 season, the two leagues combined into one big National Football League. The former leagues were split into the National Football Conference (NFC) and the American Football Conference (AFC). Today, the winners of the two conferences still meet in the Super Bowl. The Super Bowl has become the biggest single-day sporting event in the entire world.

It's not just the Super Bowl that makes football so popular. The regular season and the playoffs leading up to the big game capture the attention of fans everywhere. College football remains very popular, too. Kids as young as five or six years old compete in Pop Warner leagues. Some kids play all the way through high school. A few even go on to play in college or as pros. Let's learn a little bit about the rules of this high-impact, fast-paced game!

CHAPTER TWO

Rules

et's go back to that Yale-Princeton game in the 1870s. Football had a different look and feel. The rules were a lot different than they are today, too.

In 1875, there were 15 players on each team. Today, only 11 men play for each side at a time. There was no such thing as alternating possession or the down and distance system. Back then, whichever team had the ball simply tried to keep it out

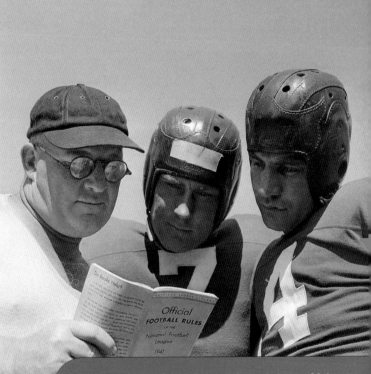

NY Giants coach Steve Owen (left) and players Mel Hein (center) and Tuffy Leemans (right) consult the NFL rule book in 1941.

of the other team's hands. It was one great big game of keep-away! Today, a team has four downs, or attempts, to move 10 yards (9.1 meters), or it must give up the ball. In the early days of the game, when one team crossed the other team's goal line, it touched the ball down to the ground to gain a point. That's now called a touchdown, which is worth six points today.

American football needed someone to step in and transform it into its own **unique** game. Walter Camp is the man responsible for creating many of the rules that gave American football its identity. His ideas set the game apart from its European **ancestors**.

Camp was the captain of the Yale football team in the late 1870s and early 1880s. He believed that the existing rules kept football from being exciting to play and watch. Camp wanted to open up the game. He wanted players to be speedy and quick, not just strong. So in 1880, he recommended some important changes to the rules. One was reducing the number of men on the field to 11 per team. Another was that each play would begin with one player (the center) snapping the ball to another (the quarterback). And, most important, he recommended that one team keep possession of the ball until it believed it could not progress any farther. Then the team would voluntarily give up the ball.

Walter Camp, shown here at Yale University in about 1878, is known as the father of American football. His brilliant ideas helped shape some of football's first rules.

Camp's idea about possession caused a problem. Teams with possession of the ball would never give up the ball! They believed that they always had a chance to move farther up the field. Teams would keep the ball sometimes for an entire half of a game. That wasn't very exciting for the players or the spectators. A couple of years later, more changes were made. Teams were required to move the ball 5 yards (4.6 m) in three plays or give up the ball. In 1912, the rule was changed to 10 yards in four plays. This new rule made sure that the game would be more fun, fair, and exciting to watch.

1924

Rules for high school, college, and professional football have changed over time. This team played for Indiana's Notre Dame University in 1924.

Camp also helped revolutionize scoring. In the early days of football, kicking awarded more points than running or passing. In the earliest days of college football, the ball was advanced only by kicking it or butting it—just like in soccer. Kicking the ball through goalposts on the end lines scored goals.

But Camp wanted a new scoring system. After some experimentation, a touchdown became worth five points in 1898. In 1909, field goals were reduced to three points, and in 1912 touchdowns became six points. Later, an extra point kick was added.

Football rules have been tweaked many times since Camp's innovations. There are also many differences between high school, college, and professional football. But Camp's vision for an exciting, competitive sport put in place the basic framework that has existed since the early 1900s.

Learning & Innovation Skills

In the NFL, the Rules Committee meets each year to discuss the rules. It decides whether any changes need to be made based on new knowledge or changing technologies. One of the biggest rule changes in recent years is the use of instant replay in reviewing decisions made by the officials. Instant replay was adopted in the late 1980s and early 1990s. At first, instant replay was limited to only a few different plays. But since 1999, the NFL has used it in certain circumstances to aid officiating. One thing that instant replay has proved is that it is effective in helping officials make better calls.

CHAPTER THREE

Equipment

No other athlete has a uniform quite like a football player. From head to toe, he is covered in equipment designed to protect him from injury. He is like an armored knight going into battle. Equipment suppliers have always searched for innovative ways to improve a player's comfort and safety.

The earliest players wore a uniform that didn't look anything like the ones worn today.

In the early 1900s, the football helmet was made of soft leather. It gave players only minimal protection. The helmets were so easy to bend that after a game, a player could simply fold up his helmet and stuff it in his pocket. Extra padding was added, but that wasn't enough.

The helmet didn't take a big leap forward until 1939. That's when Gerry E. Morgan, of the Riddell Company,

Early football uniforms featured soft leather helmets and thick pants. They didn't offer players much protection.

manufactured a plastic helmet. Unfortunately, the original helmet cracked too easily, and it was outlawed by the league. It was too dangerous to use in a game that had lots of hard hitting. So Riddell continued to improve its product, and the ban was lifted in the late 1940s. By that time, great strides had been made in the production of plastic.

Today, helmets are specially designed to help protect against **concussions**. They have come a long way from the helmets that could be folded up and stuffed in the pocket of uniform pants.

Uniform pants were originally made of heavy canvas. The jersey was a turtleneck that was made out of heavy wool. But this uniform got too hot in warm weather and too heavy in rainy weather.

Modern football helmets are made of hard plastic to help prevent head injuries. They include padding on the inside, a face mask, and a chin strap.

By the 1930s, knitted fabrics began to take the place of canvas and wool. By the 1950s, **synthetics** made the uniform much more comfortable. Today, jerseys are made from a polyester mesh. They are not only lighter than ever, but also keep players cooler when it's hot and warmer when it's cold.

When it was rainy and muddy, players complained about slipping. Their regular shoes gave them little support and traction. Riddell came up with another solution. The company began making shoes with interchangeable cleats in 1927. Those cleats provided players with better traction and support.

But safe equipment isn't everything you need to be successful on the field. Let's learn about some of the game's winning strategies.

CHAPTER FOUR

Training and Strategy

Today, football is played on fresh-cut grass or turf, both of which are safer to play on than dirt.

Have you heard the old saying, "Three yards and a cloud of dust"? Well, that was what football was like during the early days of its history. The fields were mostly dirt, with a few rocks and some gravel mixed in. There wasn't much passing, because it was illegal to throw a forward pass. Even after the forward pass was legalized in 1906, it had to be from at least 5 yards

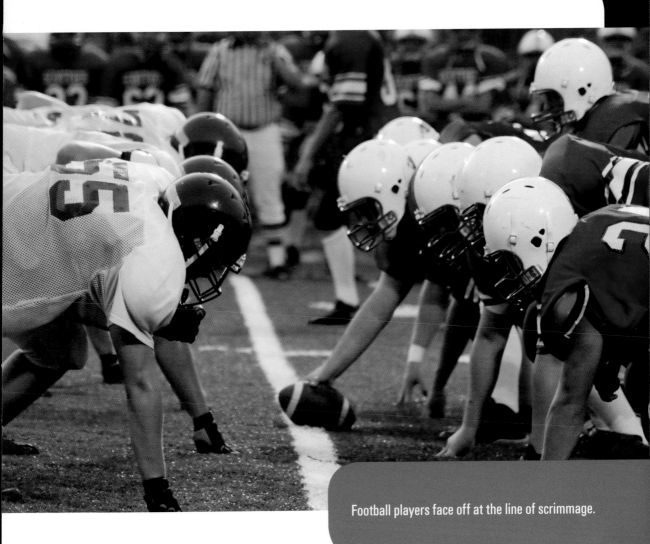

Football players face off at the line of scrimmage.

behind the line of scrimmage. (The line of scrimmage
is an imaginary line crossing the football field at the
location where the ball was placed at the end of the last
play.) Laterals, or backward passes, were allowed, but they
were risky and weren't used much.

In 1933, it became legal to throw a forward pass from anywhere behind the line of scrimmage. Many coaches still had their players run the ball. They didn't want to

Rule changes allowed players to throw the ball to other players rather than carrying it themselves. Some people think Green Bay Packers quarterback Brett Favre did it better than anyone.

take a chance with such a risky play. But the coaches who did start throwing the ball became **pioneers** and led the most successful teams.

Green Bay Packers coach Curly Lambeau was the first coach to use passing as a key play in his offensive attack. Before Lambeau, passing was used mainly as a last resort. But he had some star players in the 1930s who were good at catching the ball. Green Bay Packer Don Hutson became one of the greatest pass catchers football had ever seen. Lambeau was right to recognize the importance of the forward pass. His team won six championships between 1921 and 1949.

One of football's first big rivalries was between Lambeau's Green Bay Packers and George Halas's Chicago Bears in the 1920s and 1930s. They were the two most successful franchises of the time. Such a rivalry naturally **spurs** innovation. Competition makes everyone want to get better.

Halas was the owner of the Bears. He also coached the team for 40 years in four different 10-year periods between 1920 and 1967. He was the first coach to have his players practice every day. He believed that his players could get an upper hand on the competition by training daily. Halas was also the first coach to watch films of his opponents' games. He figured out that by doing this, he could prepare his own team ahead of time to react

to what other teams would try. The Bears won seven
football titles between 1921 and 1946.

Later on, in the 1940s and 1950s, Paul Brown, coach
of the Cleveland Browns, started grading his players'

Curly Lambeau (holding hat) coached the Green
Bay Packers to a National Football League
championship win in 1944.

performance during games. That's not a surprise—Brown was a schoolteacher before he was a football coach! Classroom study became a big part of a player's training. Today, players often spend more time in classroom and film study than they do on the practice field. Read on to learn about more of the strategies that evolved from the sport's great innovators.

The Bears' George Halas wanted to stay ahead of the competition. He decided to bring in a famous college coach named Clark Shaughnessy and former Bears coach Ralph Jones. Their job was to implement a new offense in Chicago. That offense was called the T Formation, where 3 running backs line up about 5 yards behind the quarterback. The T Formation took the NFL by storm. In 1940, Halas's Bears used the "T" to wallop the Washington Redskins 73–0 in the championship game. That is still the most lopsided game in NFL history.

By the early 1950s, every NFL team was using the T Formation. Some part of the "T" remains the basis for nearly every football team's offense today.

CHAPTER FIVE

The Innovators

George Halas, Curly Lambeau, Bear Bryant, Vince Lombardi, and Don Shula are just a few of the people who have coached teams to victory. Today, their names are legendary. Because of their out-of-the-box thinking, they helped change the game of football forever. Here are a few more of football's master innovators.

Walter Camp

Walter Camp was an American football visionary. He was the captain of the Yale University football team when he was just a sophomore in college. During his time at Yale, he was sent to represent the university at the important national rules convention in 1877.

After graduating, Camp went on to become a football coach. He also worked as a sportswriter. He continued to serve on the national Rules Committee for nearly half a century. It was his innovative rule changes that helped turn American football into a unique game. Camp helped football separate itself from soccer and rugby. He also was the first man to name an "All-America" football team. For his role in the evolution and spread of the game, Camp is often called the Father of American Football.

Amos Alonzo Stagg

Legendary college coach Knute Rockne once said, "All football comes from Stagg." That may be an exaggeration, but only a slight one. That's because much

Before becoming head coach at the University of Chicago, Amos Alonzo Stagg was a star player at Yale University in Connecticut.

of what is taken for granted in the game today was started and popularized by Stagg.

Stagg was the head coach at the University of Chicago for 41 years beginning in 1892. He turned the school into a powerhouse in the Big 10 with his innovative methods in games and in practice. On the field, he would have his players gather in a huddle before each snap to call the play. Stagg introduced the man in motion, a concept that confused opposing defenses. In practice, he had his players train with the use of a tackling dummy. He was the first coach to have his players wear jersey numbers. Before becoming a coach, Stagg was one of the first star players. He was an end on Walter Camp's first All-America team in 1889.

Paul Brown

Each year, prospective NFL draft picks take a special version of an IQ test. That was originally Paul Brown's idea. Every NFL team sends its plays in from the sidelines. That was Brown's idea, too. Classroom study? Yep, his idea. Playbooks? Check. Face masks? Check.

Brown not only introduced many innovations to the NFL, he was also a pretty good coach. His Cleveland Browns—the team that was named after him—played in 10 consecutive championship games from 1946 to 1955.

The Cleveland Browns won seven of them. In 1968,
Brown founded and coached the Cincinnati Bengals.

Paul Brown (wearing baseball cap) led the
Cleveland Browns to seven league championships.
He was an innovative coach with many new ideas.

Bill Walsh

Bill Walsh was the highly successful coach of the San Francisco 49ers from 1979 to 1988. He is often credited as being the one who created the "West Coast Offense." But Walsh insists that he was really just building on things he learned working for other innovators such as Paul Brown (Cincinnati) and Sid Gillman (San Diego).

San Francisco 49ers coach Bill Walsh is hoisted on the shoulders of his team after beating the Miami Dolphins in the Super Bowl in January 1985. He died in 2007.

It is more accurate to say that Walsh popularized the offense. The West Coast Offense is a difficult offensive strategy. It relies on short, high-percentage passes (short passes that are most often completed) and precise timing routes between a quarterback and his receivers.

What made Walsh so inventive was how he used the offense. For many years, NFL coaches used a running attack to set up a passing play. Walsh was the first coach to use the pass to control the ball and set up the run.

Walsh helped carry the 49ers to three Super Bowl wins in his 10 seasons as head coach. And because so many of his assistants went on to become NFL head coaches, the majority of teams use some form of the West Coast Offense today.

Life & Career Skills

Paul Brown was Bill Walsh's **mentor**. In 1975, Brown retired as coach of the Cincinnati Bengals. Walsh, who was an assistant coach in Cincinnati, was disappointed when he was passed over to succeed Brown as head coach. So Walsh had a decision to make. Should he stay in Cincinnati and work for someone else? Or should he go elsewhere to pursue his dream of becoming an NFL head coach? It was the kind of tough choice that people in all sorts of jobs sometimes have to make. In the end, Walsh decided to move on. It turned out to be the right choice. He became one of pro football's greatest coaches with the San Francisco 49ers.

What would you do if you felt you were unfairly passed over for a promotion?

Glossary

amateur (AM-uh-chur) a person who does something without getting paid for doing it

ancestors (AN-sess-turz) people who came earlier in the family line

concussions (kuhn-KUSH-uhnz) blows to the head that impair the function of the brain

innovations (ihn-uh-VAY-shuhnz) new things or new ways of thinking

media (MEE-dee-uh) the men and women who report about events for newspapers, radio, television, and the Internet

mentor (MEN-tohr) someone who teaches or advises a younger or more inexperienced person

pioneers (pye-uh-NEERZ) people who lead the way for others by becoming the first to accomplish something

professional (pruh-FESH-uh-nuhl) describing a sport that is played for money or as a career

spurs (SPURZ) urges to action

synthetics (sin-THET-iks) items produced chemically, instead of from natural origin

unique (yoo-NEEK) one of a kind

For More Information

Books

Buckley, James, Jr. *The Child's World Encyclopedia of the NFL*. Mankato, MN: The Child's World, 2007.

Christopher, Matt. *The Super Bowl: Legendary Sports Events*. New York: Little Brown Young Readers, 2006.

Pellowski, Michael J. *A Little Giant Book: Football Facts*. New York: Sterling, 2007.

Web Sites

Fact Monster
www.factmonster.com/sports.html
Click on the football tab for lots of facts and figures about college and pro football, the Super Bowl, and much more

NFL Rush
www.nflrush.com
Find lots of games and contests, and information about your favorite players and teams

Sports Illustrated for Kids
www.siforkids.com
Click on the "NFL" or "NCAA Football" tabs to get information on pro or college football

Index

About the Author

Jim Gigliotti is a freelance writer who lives in Southern California with his wife and two children. A former editor at NFL Publishing, he has written more than two dozen books for youngsters and adults, including *Stadium Stories: USC Trojans* and biographies on football stars Tom Brady, Peyton Manning, and LaDainian Tomlinson.